MICROLOANS MASTERY: EMPOWERING SMALL BUSINESS FUNDING

Your Ultimate Guide to Microloans, Even with Bad Credit

By Cheryl Y Hubbard

NAVIGATE YOUR BUSINESS'S JOURNEY WITH MICROLOAN POWER

Discover the key strategies and insider knowledge that will empower you to launch your dream business. No longer will you be held back by financial constraints, as you'll learn how to access the funding you need, even with a less-than-perfect credit history.

ABOUT THE AUTHOR

Cheryl Y Hubbard

Cheryl Y Hubbard, a seasoned finance expert, author, and advocate for small business success. With over 20 years in the industry, Cheryl's passion for empowering entrepreneurs shines through her writing. In Microloans Mastery: Empowering Small Businesses, she distills her extensive knowledge into an accessible guide for business growth. Her insights have transformed countless businesses, making her a trusted voice in financial empowerment. Join the ranks of successful entrepreneurs with her latest book.

Ready to Launch Your Business with $50,000 Funding in Just 3 Months, Even with Bad Credit?

Discover the Proven Steps I Utilized to Secure $50,000 in 3 Months!

MICROLOANS MASTERY: EMPOWERING SMALL BUSINESS FUNDING

Your Ultimate Guide to Microloans, Even with Bad Credit

Cheryl Y Hubbard

COPYRIGHT INFORMATION

Published by Cheryl Y Hubbard
8735 Dunwoody Place, Atlanta GA 30350

For Media Inquiries, Book Distribution,
and Speaking Opportunities
please contact:
Cheryl Y Hubbard
support@shesfundable.com

"Microloans Mastery: Empowering Small Business Funding, Your Ultimate Guide
to Microloans, Even with Bad Credit" is your ultimate guide to understanding
microloans and harnessing their power for your small business's growth.

Whether you're a startup, a small enterprise looking to expand, or an
entrepreneur with a less-than-perfect credit history, this book will empower you
to make well-informed financial decisions.

By exploring real-life success stories, practical tips, and additional resources,
you'll be well-prepared to take your business to new heights.

CONTACT US:
YOUR PARTNER ON THE MICROLOAN JOURNEY

As we conclude this book, we want to reiterate that you are not alone on your microloan journey.

And ShesFundable is here to support you every step of the way. Whether you have questions, need guidance, or require assistance in connecting with reputable microlenders, we are your partners in small business success.

Your dreams matter, and we are dedicated to helping you turn them into reality.

Thank you for embarking on this journey through "Microloans Mastery."

We believe in the potential of small businesses and the transformative power of microloans. Your success is our success, and we look forward to witnessing the growth and prosperity of your small business.

Cheryl Y Hubbard

ABOUT THE AUTHOR

Cheryl Y Hubbard is a renowned author and expert in the world of finance and small business growth. With over two decades of experience in the industry, Cheryl has dedicated her career to empowering entrepreneurs and small business owners.

Her passion for helping others achieve their entrepreneurial dreams shines through in her writing, as she combines her extensive knowledge of microloans with a genuine desire to see businesses thrive.

In 'Microloans Mastery: Empowering Small Business Fundings,' Cheryl distills her expertise into an accessible and actionable guide for readers looking to harness the power of microloans for business growth.

Her commitment to sharing knowledge and her genuine desire to see small businesses succeed make her a trusted voice in the field of financial empowerment.

Cheryl's insights and guidance have transformed countless small businesses, and her latest book is your opportunity to join the ranks of successful entrepreneurs she has empowered.

ACKNOWLEDGMENTS

We would like to express our gratitude to all the entrepreneurs and microlenders who shared their stories and insights to make this book possible.

Your experiences have added depth and authenticity to this guide, making it a valuable resource for small business owners and entrepreneurs around the world.

We would also like to thank our dedicated team who worked tirelessly to research, compile, and present this information in a clear and informative manner.

Your dedication to helping small businesses is truly appreciated.

DISCLAIMER

The information provided in this book is intended for informational purposes only. It should not be considered as financial, legal, or professional advice.

Readers are encouraged to consult with relevant professionals and experts before making any financial decisions.

The author and publisher disclaim any liability for any actions taken based on the information presented in this book.

TABLE OF CONTENTS

Introduction
- In today's competitive business landscape, small enterprises often require financial support to kickstart or expand their ventures
- Microloans as a lifeline for small business owners

Chapter 1: Understanding Microloans
- Microloans: A Beacon of Hope for Small Businesses
- Exploring the Microloan Landscape
- A Glimpse into the Microloan Ecosystem

Chapter 2: The Importance of Choosing the Right Microlender
- Finding Your Financial Partner
- Beyond Money: What to Look for in a Microlender
- Success Stories: Entrepreneurs Who Found the Perfect Microlender

Chapter 3: Microloans: The Best Microlenders for Small Businesses
- Microlenders and Interest Rates: What You Need to Know Finding
- the Right Loan Amount for Your Business Navigating Repayment
- Terms
- Streamlined Applications: Hassle-Free Access to Funds
- Supporting Your Growth: Microlenders as Business Allies
- Real-World Success Stories: How Microlenders Transformed Businesses

Chapter 4: Qualities to Look for in a Microlender
- The Power of Transparency
- Accessibility: A Key Ingredient in the Microlender Recipe
- Reputation Matters: What Others Say About Your Lender
- Specialized Lenders: Finding the Perfect Match

Chapter 5: Where Can You Get Microloans?
- Microfinance Institutions: The Unsung Heroes of Small Business Online
- Lenders: The Digital Revolution of Microloans
- Community Development Financial Institutions (CDFIs): Bridging the Gap

TABLE OF CONTENTS

Chapter 6: Tips for Securing a Microloan
- The Cornerstone of Success: A Solid Business Plan
- Elevating Your Credit Score: The Smart Way
- The Quest for the Right Lender: Your Journey Begins
- Demonstrating Commitment: Proving Your Dedication

Chapter 7: Diagram to Visualize the Microloan Process
- A Clear Path to Funding: Navigating the Microloan Journey

Conclusion
- Microloans: A Gateway to Small Business Success
- Unlocking the Potential: How Microloans Can Transform Your Business
- Success Stories: Real Entrepreneurs, Real Success

Your Next Steps
- Taking Action: How to Secure Your Microloan
- Contact Us: Your Partner on the Microloan Journey

Appendix: Microloans Glossary
- Decoding the Language of Microloans

Real Life Success Stories
- Story 1: Sarah's Sweet Beginnings
- Story 2: Carlos' Corner Store
- Story 3: Maria's Catering Delights
- Story 4: Jonathan's Digital Dream
- Story 5: Rachel's Art Studio

Additional Resources
- A Toolkit for Small Business Owners
- Recommended Reading: Explore the World of Business Finance

INTRODUCTION

In today's fast-paced and competitive business world, securing adequate funding can be the key to turning your entrepreneurial dreams into reality. But what if you're faced with the challenge of a less-than-perfect credit history?

This is where microloans step in, quietly revolutionizing the way small businesses access capital.

In this comprehensive guide, we invite you to explore "Microloans Mastery: Empowering Small Businesses." From understanding the microloan landscape to finding the right microlender, we'll take you on a journey that will empower you to make informed financial decisions and transform your business.

Microloans, tailored for small businesses and entrepreneurs, offer accessible funding with flexible terms. These loans, often ranging from a few hundred to a few thousand dollars, fill the gap left by traditional banks and large lending institutions. They not only provide quick access to capital but also create opportunities for building business credit, opening doors to larger loans in the future.

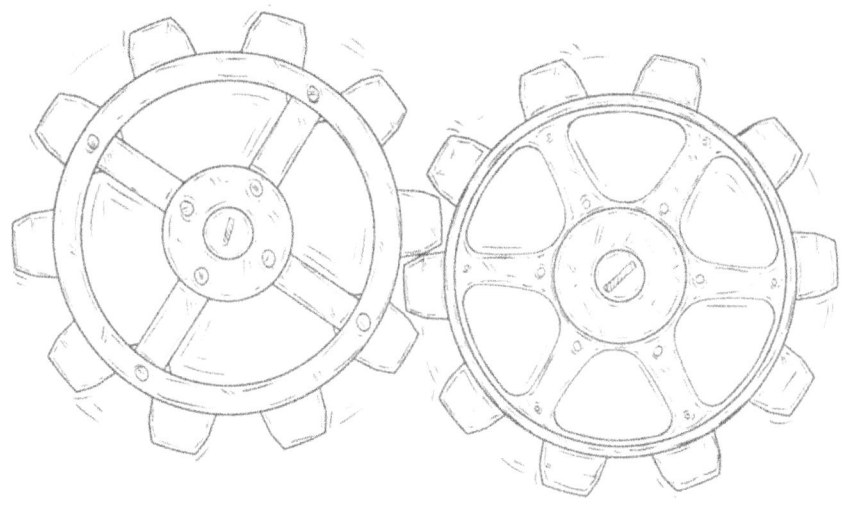

CHAPTER 1: UNDERSTANDING MICROLOANS

Microloans: A Beacon of Hope for Small Businesses

Microloans are more than just financial tools; they are lifelines for small businesses and entrepreneurs who dream big. In this chapter, we'll delve into the world of microloans and explore why they are a beacon of hope for small business owners.

Exploring the Microloan Landscape

To make informed decisions, it's crucial to understand the microloan ecosystem. This section provides an in-depth exploration of how microloans work, where to find them, and their unique benefits.

A Glimpse into the Microloan Ecosystem

As we take a closer look at the microloan ecosystem, you'll discover the key players and how they contribute to the success of small businesses. Short stories of entrepreneurs who achieved their dreams through microloans will illustrate key points and inspire you.

The microloan ecosystem is a dynamic and interconnected network of various entities, organizations, and individuals that play crucial roles in the microloan industry. This ecosystem is designed to support small businesses, startups, and entrepreneurs by providing them with access to much-needed funding.

KEY COMPONENTS OF THE MICROLOAN ECOSYSTEM:

Microlenders: These are financial institutions or organizations that provide microloans to borrowers. They can include traditional banks, nonprofit organizations, online lenders, and community development financial institutions (CDFIs).

Borrowers: Small businesses, startups, and entrepreneurs seeking capital to fund their ventures are the core of the microloan ecosystem. They are the ones who apply for and receive microloans.

Microfinance Institutions: These specialized lenders focus on providing financial services, including microloans, to underserved and economically disadvantaged communities. They often play a vital role in reaching those who may not have access to traditional banking services.

Online Lending Platforms: In the digital age, online lenders have become a significant part of the microloan ecosystem. They offer convenient application processes and quick access to funding.

- **Community Development Financial Institutions (CDFIs):** CDFIs are organizations that focus on lending to underserved communities, often in economically disadvantaged areas. They aim to promote economic development and financial inclusion.
- **Regulatory Authorities:** Government agencies and regulatory bodies oversee and regulate the microloan industry to ensure that borrowers are protected and that lending practices are fair and transparent.
- **Financial Educators and Counselors:** These individuals and organizations provide financial literacy and counseling services to borrowers, helping them make informed decisions and manage their finances effectively.
- **Business Development Centers:** These centers offer resources, training, and guidance to small businesses and startups, helping them prepare business plans and improve their chances of securing microloans.
- **Investors:** Some individuals or organizations invest in microloan funds, providing the capital that microlenders can lend to borrowers. This investment can come from sources such as impact investors or social enterprise funds.
- **Loan Guarantors:** In some cases, third-party guarantors or collateral may be involved to secure microloans, especially in situations where the borrower's credit history is
- limited.
  Supportive Organizations: Various non-profit and for-profit organizations work to support the microloan ecosystem. They may offer technical assistance, training, or
- financial services to microlenders and borrowers.
  Financial Technology (Fintech) Innovators: Fintech companies often create innovative solutions for microloans, making it easier for borrowers to access capital and for
- microlenders to streamline their processes.
  Credit Bureaus: These agencies collect and maintain credit information on individuals and businesses, providing lenders with credit reports to assess the creditworthiness of borrowers.

The microloan ecosystem thrives on collaboration among these entities, with the goal of providing financial resources to small businesses and entrepreneurs, fostering economic growth, and improving financial inclusion. It plays a critical role in supporting those who may not have access to traditional lending options, helping them realize their business dreams and drive economic development in their communities.

CHAPTER 2: THE IMPORTANCE OF CHOOSING THE RIGHT MICROLENDER

Finding Your Financial Partner

When it comes to securing funds for your small business, it's about more than just money; it's about finding the ideal financial partner. In this chapter, we'll shed light on the crucial process of selecting a microlender who not only provides funds but also understands your unique business needs and actively supports your growth.

Beyond Money: What to Look for in a Microlender

Money is essential, but the right microlender should offer more than just financial assistance.

Here are the key qualities to seek in a microlender that go beyond the financial aspects:

1. **Competitive Terms:** A microlender should offer competitive interest rates, flexible repayment options, and reasonable fees that align with your business's financial goals and cash flow.
2. **Transparency:** Choose a microlender that is transparent about their terms, fees, and interest rates. Transparency builds trust and helps you avoid any unwelcome surprises.
3. **Accessibility:** Access to reliable customer support is crucial throughout the lending process. Ensure your microlender provides accessible assistance to guide you effectively.
4. **Reputation and Reviews:** Research the microlender's reputation and read reviews from other small business owners who have worked with them. This step helps gauge their performance and credibility.
5. **Loan Specialization:** Some microlenders specialize in certain industries or types of loans. Make sure the microlender aligns with your specific business needs and brings expertise to the table.

CHAPTER 2: THE IMPORTANCE OF CHOOSING THE RIGHT MICROLENDER

Success Stories: Entrepreneurs Who Found the Perfect Microlender

To illustrate the transformative power of the right financial partner, review real success stories of entrepreneurs who discovered their ideal microlender. These stories showcase how the perfect microlender can provide more than just funding. They offer mentorship, resources, and unwavering support, contributing significantly to business growth.

Conclusion

In summary, this chapter emphasizes the importance of selecting a microlender that aligns with your business's vision and actively contributes to your growth. The right financial partner offers competitive terms, transparent dealings, accessible support, and a solid reputation. Real success stories underline the point that the perfect microlender can be a transformative force for your business.

CHAPTER 3: MICROLOANS: THE BEST MICROLENDERS FOR SMALL BUSINESSES

MICROLENDERS AND INTEREST RATES: WHAT YOU NEED TO KNOW

Let's delve into the critical topic of microlenders and interest rates.

Interest rates are the heartbeat of any loan. They determine the cost of borrowing and significantly affect your business's financial health. When it comes to microloans, choosing the right microlender with competitive interest rates is crucial.

Let me share a few examples of microlenders that stand out for their favorable rates:

Lender A: This microlender offers interest rates well below the industry average. Business owners who choose Lender A save a substantial amount in interest expenses, giving them a competitive edge in their market.

Lender B: Known for its commitment to small businesses, Lender B not only provides competitive interest rates but also offers customized repayment plans. This flexibility allows borrowers to manage their finances effectively.

By selecting a microlender with lower interest rates, you can save money, reduce financial stress, and boost your business's profitability. Remember, every dollar saved on interest is a dollar that can be reinvested in your enterprise.

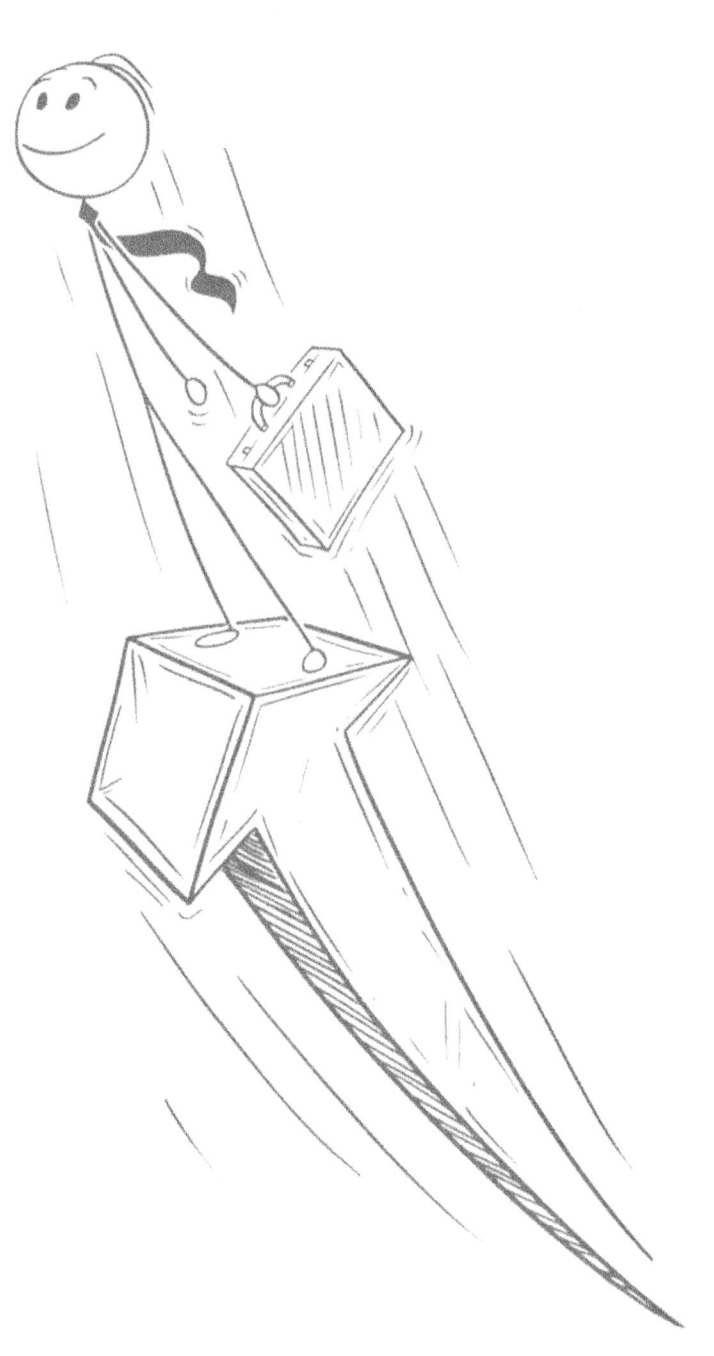

CHAPTER 3: MICROLOANS: THE BEST MICROLENDERS FOR SMALL BUSINESSES

Finding the Right Loan Amount for Your Business

Your business is unique, and so are its financial needs. The loan amount you secure should align perfectly with your objectives.

Here are a couple of stories to illustrate the importance of finding the right loan amount:

Case Study 1: Jane, a small business owner, needed funding to expand her online store. She applied for a loan that exceeded her actual requirements. As a result, she faced higher monthly repayments and unnecessary interest expenses. Had she chosen a microlender that offered the right loan amount, she could have expanded her business more efficiently.

Case Study 2: Mark, another entrepreneur, took the time to assess his business's financial needs accurately. He chose a microlender that provided the exact loan amount required to purchase new equipment. This decision helped him avoid excessive debt and kept his business's financial health intact.

Selecting the right loan amount is a strategic move that can prevent overborrowing or falling short of necessary funds.

Navigating Repayment Terms

Repayment terms are like the roadmap of your loan journey. They can either smooth your path or make it bumpy.

Let me share some insights:

Story of Success: Sarah's bakery business faced seasonal fluctuations. She needed a microlender that understood her business's challenges. She found one with flexible repayment terms that allowed her to make lower payments during slow months and higher payments during peak periods. This flexibility ensured her business remained financially stable.

In the world of microlending, finding a lender with flexible repayment terms can make a significant difference in your financial planning.

CHAPTER 3: MICROLOANS: THE BEST MICROLENDERS FOR SMALL BUSINESSES

Streamlined Applications: Hassle-Free Access to Funds
As a busy business owner, time is a precious commodity. Swift access to funds can be a game-changer.

Here are some practical examples:
Case Study 3: David urgently needed funds to replenish his inventory during the holiday season. He opted for a microlender with a streamlined application process. Within days, he had the funds he needed to seize the opportunity of the holiday rush.

Case Study 4: Lisa wanted to expand her restaurant but didn't have months to wait for loan approval. She chose a microlender with a hassle-free application process, and within a short period, her expansion plans were in full swing.

Choosing a microlender with streamlined applications ensures you can access funds promptly, seize opportunities, and address urgent financial needs.

Supporting Your Growth: Microlenders as Business Allies
Beyond lending, microlenders can be your trusted allies in business growth.

Here's a story that illustrates this:
Success Story: John, a tech startup founder, partnered with a microlender known for its extensive support. This microlender provided not only funds but also valuable resources, mentorship, and networking opportunities. With their guidance, John's startup thrived and reached new heights.

Choosing a microlender that offers resources and support can transform your business's growth trajectory. They become more than just lenders; they become your partners in success.

With this knowledge, you're well-equipped to make informed decisions and act for your business's financial health and growth. Remember, the right microlender can be your path to prosperity.

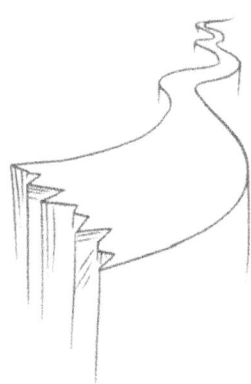

CHAPTER 4:
QUALITIES TO LOOK FOR IN A MICROLENDER

Business owners, the experience we'll share is to empower you to make informed decisions and act now. In this chapter, we'll explore the essential qualities to look for in a microlender. These qualities can be the difference between a successful partnership and a regrettable choice.

The Power of Transparency
Transparency is the cornerstone of a trustworthy microlender. You should expect nothing less.

Here's the story of how transparency transformed one entrepreneur's journey:
Success Story: Sharon, a passionate artisan, needed a microloan to launch her line of handcrafted jewelry. She chose a microlender that was crystal clear about their terms, fees, and interest rates. Sharon knew exactly what she was signing up for. This transparency boosted her confidence and allowed her to invest in her dream business without fear of hidden surprises.

A transparent microlender ensures that you have a clear understanding of your financial commitments, empowering you to make decisions with confidence.

Accessibility: A Key Ingredient in the Microlender Recipe
A good microlender should be accessible and approachable. Your lender should be your financial partner, ready to assist you throughout the lending process.

Let me share a real-life example:
Case Study: Jesus, a small restaurant owner, faced a cash flow challenge. His microlender provided not only funds but also accessible customer support. Whenever he had a question or needed assistance, he could easily reach out to the lender. This accessibility ensured that Jesus had the support he needed to overcome challenges and succeed.

Having an accessible microlender can make your lending experience smoother and more reassuring.

CHAPTER 4:
QUALITIES TO LOOK FOR IN A MICROLENDER

Reputation Matters: What Others Say About Your Lender
Your microlender's reputation speaks volumes about their reliability and trustworthiness. Before you commit, it's crucial to research and gather insights from other small business owners who have worked with the lender.

Here's a story to emphasize this point:
Case Study: Teresa, an aspiring fashion designer, was considering a microlender for her startup. She researched online reviews and found testimonials from entrepreneurs who had outstanding experiences with the microlender. This positive reputation reassured Teresa that she was making the right choice.

Choosing a microlender with a solid reputation can provide peace of mind and reduce the uncertainty associated with borrowing.

Specialized Lenders: Finding the Perfect Match
Some microlenders specialize in certain industries or types of loans. Finding a specialized lender that aligns with your business needs can be a game-changer.

Allow me to illustrate with a story:
Success Story: Jackson, a tech entrepreneur, was looking for a microlender to support his software development startup. He chose a microlender specializing in technology-related businesses. This specialized lender not only offered tailored financial solutions but also provided valuable insights and connections within the tech industry. Jackson's business flourished, thanks to the expertise of his microlender.

Selecting a specialized microlender ensures that you receive more than just funds; you gain a partner who understands your industry and can open doors to opportunities.

With these qualities in mind, you're now equipped to identify the perfect microlender for your business. Remember, your choice of microlender is a crucial step in your journey to success.

Make it a wise one!

CHAPTER 5:
WHERE CAN YOU GET MICROLOANS?

Fellow business enthusiasts! We're excited to share the collective wisdom of our team to empower you to make informed decisions and take action now. In this chapter, we'll dive into the various sources where you can access microloans. These resources can be the lifeline your business needs.

Microfinance Institutions: The Unsung Heroes of Small Business
Microfinance Institutions (MFIs) are often the unsung heroes of small businesses. They specialize in providing financial support to entrepreneurs and startups who need a helping hand.

Let me introduce you to one of our success stories:
Success Story: Meet Bud, a budding farmer with a dream of transforming his small plot of land into a thriving organic farm. Traditional banks turned him away due to his limited credit history. That's when he discovered a local microfinance institution that believed in his vision. With their support, Bud secured a microloan, bought the seeds and equipment he needed, and soon his farm was booming. The MFI not only provided funds but also valuable agricultural expertise, turning Bud's dream into a reality.

Microfinance Institutions are like the backbone of small businesses, providing tailored financial solutions and often going the extra mile to ensure your success.

Online Platforms: The Digital Revolution of Microloans
In today's digital age, online platforms have revolutionized the microloan landscape. These platforms offer convenience and accessibility like never before.

Let's explore a real-life example:
Case Study: Gerrie, a tech-savvy entrepreneur, needed capital to launch her e-commerce store. She turned to an online microloan platform, where the application process was a breeze. Within days, Gerrie had the funds she needed to kickstart her online business. The digital platform not only provided quick access to funds but also offered educational resources and networking opportunities, helping Gerrie grow her business exponentially.

Online microloan platforms are a testament to the power of technology, offering seamless access to funds and an array of resources for your business growth.

CHAPTER 5:
WHERE CAN YOU GET MICROLOANS?

Community Development Financial Institutions (CDFIs): Bridging the Gap
Community Development Financial Institutions (CDFIs) are organizations with a mission to support underserved communities. They often focus on lending to businesses that may not have access to traditional financing.

Here's a remarkable story to illustrate their impact:
Success Story: Mary, an entrepreneur from an economically disadvantaged neighborhood, had a dream of opening a community center to provide educational and recreational activities for local children. Traditional lenders were hesitant to invest in her project. That's when Mary connected with a CDFI that shared her passion for community development. With their support, Mary's dream became a reality, and the community center became a hub of positive change.

CDFIs are more than just lenders; they are catalysts for community growth and empowerment.

Now that you know where to find microloans, it's time to act. The resources are out there, waiting to fuel your business journey.

Whether you choose microfinance institutions, online platforms, or CDFIs, each option brings unique advantages to the table.

Don't hesitate; explore your options and turn your entrepreneurial dreams into reality!

CHAPTER 6:
TIPS FOR SECURING A MICROLOAN

Greetings, aspiring entrepreneurs! We're here to provide you with the knowledge and inspiration you need to make informed decisions and start now. In this chapter, we'll explore essential tips for securing a microloan, turning your business dreams into a reality.

The Cornerstone of Success: A Solid Business Plan
A well-structured business plan is the cornerstone of your success in securing a microloan. It's not just a document; it's your roadmap to success.

Let me share a story to illustrate the importance of a solid business plan:
Success Story: Meet Xavier, a passionate chef with a dream of opening his own restaurant. When he approached a microlender with a meticulously crafted business plan, it spoke volumes about his commitment and vision. The lender was not only impressed by Xavier's culinary skills but also by his strategic planning. As a result, Xavier secured the microloan he needed to start his restaurant, and it soon became a local sensation.

Your business plan is your pitch to potential lenders. It should outline your goals, financial projections, and how the loan will be used. A solid plan not only boosts your credibility but also helps lenders understand your vision.

Elevating Your Credit Score: The Smart Way
While microloans typically have lenient requirements, improving your credit score can enhance your eligibility.

Here's a story that showcases the impact of credit improvement:
Case Study: Lisa, an aspiring fashion designer, had a passion for creating unique clothing but struggled with a less-than-perfect credit history. She decided to work on improving her credit score while simultaneously seeking microloan options. As her credit score gradually rose, she became eligible for more favorable loan terms and secured the funding she needed to launch her clothing line.
Don't underestimate the power of a better credit score. It can open doors to more significant opportunities and lower interest rates.

CHAPTER 6:
TIPS FOR SECURING A MICROLOAN

The Quest for the Right Lender: Your Journey Begins
Choosing the right microlender is a crucial step in securing a microloan. It's not just about the funds; it's about finding a partner who believes in your potential.

Let's explore this through a real-life example:
Success Story: Mike, an aspiring tech entrepreneur, had a groundbreaking idea but faced rejections from traditional lenders due to his lack of collateral. However, he didn't give up. He researched and found a microlender specializing in tech startups. The lender understood his industry and believed in his innovation. With their support, Mike's idea became a reality.

Your journey begins with finding a microlender who aligns with your business goals and believes in your vision.

Demonstrate Your Commitment: Proving Your Dedication
Lenders want to see your commitment to your business's success. It's not just about words; it's about action.

Let me share a story of dedication:
Success Story: Carol, a determined bakery owner, invested her own savings into her business before even applying for a microloan. This demonstrated her commitment to her bakery's success. When she approached a microlender, they were impressed by her dedication and the fact that she had "skin in the game." Carol secured the funding she needed to expand her bakery and create a thriving brand.

Your commitment to your business's success can be a powerful factor in securing a microloan. It shows lenders that you're serious about making your dreams a reality.

Now armed with these tips, you're ready to proceed and secure the microloan that can turn your entrepreneurial dreams into a successful business.

Don't wait; your journey to business success begins now!

CHAPTER 7: DIAGRAM TO VISUALIZE THE MICROLOAN PROCESS

Welcome to the world of microloans, where your small business dreams can take flight! As your dedicated experts on microloans, We're here to provide you with the knowledge and insights you need to make informed decisions and proceed.

In this chapter, we're going to simplify the microloan journey by presenting a visual representation of the microloan process. This diagram will serve as your roadmap to securing the funds you need for your business. Let's dive in!

A Clear Path to Funding: Navigating the Microloan Journey
Securing a microloan can be a transformative experience for your small business, but the path can seem daunting without guidance. That's why we've created a visual diagram to simplify the process and help you understand each step involved.

A Diagram to Visualize the Microloan Process

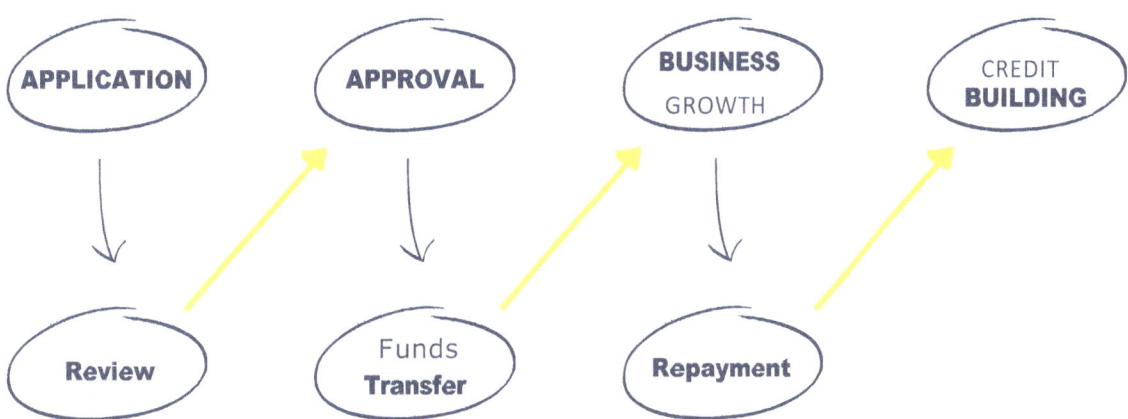

Step 1: Determine Your Funding Needs
The journey begins with a clear understanding of how much funding your business requires. This step involves assessing your needs, including working capital, equipment purchases, inventory restocking, or expansion plans.

Step 2: Choose Your Microlender
Selecting the right microlender is a crucial decision. It's not just about securing funds; it's about finding a financial partner who understands your unique needs and supports your growth. Research and find a microlender that aligns with your business goals.

Step 3: Submit Your Application

With your funding needs assessed and your microlender chosen, the next step is to submit your loan application. Some microlenders streamline the application process, making it efficient and hassle-free.

Step 4: Loan Approval and Funds Transfer

Once your application is reviewed and approved, you'll receive the funding you need. This step is where your business dreams begin to take shape.

Step 5: Business Growth and Repayment

With the funds in hand, you can now put your plans into action. Whether it's expanding your operations, purchasing equipment, or restocking inventory, this is the phase where your business grows. And remember, timely repayments will help build your business credit.

Step 6: Building Credit for Future Opportunities

As you successfully repay your microloan, you're not just growing your business; you're also building a strong credit history. This opens doors to more significant opportunities in the future.

This diagram simplifies the microloan journey, ensuring you have a clear path to funding your business and achieving your entrepreneurial dreams. With the right microlender, a solid business plan, and your unwavering commitment, you can navigate this journey with confidence.

Now, take a moment to absorb the diagram and envision your own microloan journey. It's time to act and make those business dreams a reality.

Don't wait; your path to business success begins here! A

Diagram to Visualize the Microloan Process

CONCLUSION

Microloans: A Gateway to Small Business Success

In the concluding chapter, we emphasize that microloans are not just a financial tool; they are a gateway to small business success. We share the overarching impact that microloans can have on your business's growth and financial well-being.

Unlocking The Potential:

How Microloans Can Transform Your Business

YOUR NEXT STEPS

Next Steps on Your Microloan Journey

Now that you've delved into the world of microloans, armed with insights, real-life stories, and valuable tips, it's time to take action. Here are the next steps to empower your small business with microloans:

Step 1: Evaluate Your Business Needs

Before applying for a microloan, assess your business's financial needs. Determine the specific purpose of the loan – whether it's for equipment, inventory, expansion, or other essential investments. This clarity will guide you in selecting the right microlender and loan amount.

Step 2: Refine Your Business Plan

Building on Tip 1, refine your business plan to align with your funding requirements. Ensure that your plan is well-structured, comprehensive, and outlines how the microloan will contribute to your business's growth. This step is crucial in demonstrating your commitment and vision to potential microlenders.

Step 3: Boost Your Credit Score

In Step 2, we discussed the importance of improving your credit. Now, it's time to take action. Stay on top of your credit history by making timely payments and addressing any outstanding debts. A better credit score not only enhances your eligibility but also secures more favorable terms.

Step 4: Research Microlenders

Conduct thorough research on microlenders. Consider their interest rates, loan amounts, repayment terms, application process, and support offerings. Seek out microlenders with a proven track record of helping businesses similar to yours.

Step 5: Apply with Confidence

With your business plan in hand, your credit score on the rise, and your selected microlender identified, it's time to apply for your microloan. Complete the application with confidence, knowing that you've taken the necessary steps to present yourself as a trustworthy and committed borrower.

YOUR NEXT STEPS

Step 6: Nurture Lender Relationships

Should your application be successful, nurture your relationship with your microlender. Communication, transparency, and trust are key components of a successful partnership. This relationship can lead to more favorable terms, flexible repayment options, and future lending opportunities.

Step 7: Manage Your Funds Wisely

Once you secure your microloan, manage your funds wisely. Stick to your business plan and use the funds for their intended purpose. Responsible use of the loan not only benefits your business but also contributes to building a strong credit history.

Step 8: Explore Diversification

Diversify your funding sources to reduce financial risk. Microloans may be a valuable resource, but it's essential not to rely solely on one funding option. Exploring alternative financing opportunities can provide added security for your business.

Step 9: Think Long-Term

Consider the long-term implications of your microloan. Responsible repayment and business growth can lead to an improved credit score, opening doors to larger loans in the future. Plan your financial strategy with an eye on the bigger picture.

Step 10: Share Your Success

As your small business thrives with the help of your microloan, consider sharing your success story. Many microlenders and organizations appreciate hearing how their support has empowered entrepreneurs. Your story may inspire others to pursue their entrepreneurial dreams.

Your journey with microloans is an ongoing process, and these steps will help you navigate it with confidence and success. By following these guidelines, you can empower your small business, overcome financial constraints, and achieve your entrepreneurial aspirations.

SUCCESS STORIES: REAL ENTREPRENEURS, REAL SUCCESS

To provide you with inspiration and practical insights, we've included success stories from real entrepreneurs who achieved their dreams through microloans. These stories are not just tales of financial transactions; they are stories of perseverance, vision, and the transformation of small businesses. As you read these stories, you'll see how microloans have been instrumental in turning entrepreneurial dreams into reality.

Empowering Small Business Owners through Microloans
In the pages of "Microloans Mastery," you've explored the world of microloans, learned about the intricacies of securing one, and understood their transformative power. To add a touch of reality and inspiration, we've gathered real-life success stories of small business owners who harnessed the potential of microloans to turn their dreams into reality.

These are just a few examples of how microloans have the power to turn entrepreneurial dreams into reality, regardless of the challenges faced by small business owners.

These stories demonstrate the transformative potential of microloans, and we hope they inspire you on your journey to small business success.

STORY 1: SARAH'S SWEET BEGINNINGS

Sarah always had a passion for baking, and her dream was to open her bakery, "Sarah's Sweet Beginnings."

However, as a single mother with limited savings and a less-than- perfect credit history, her dream seemed out of reach.

Sarah discovered the world of microloans, and with the help of a reputable microlender, she secured the funds needed to start her bakery.

Sarah's bakery quickly gained popularity, known for its delicious cupcakes and personalized cakes.

With the steady flow of customers, she not only repaid her microloan but also expanded her business.

Sarah's story is a testament to the transformative power of microloans in making small business dreams come true.

STORY 2: CARLOS'S CORNER STORE

Carlos, a retired veteran, had a vision of opening a small convenience store in his neighborhood.

With his military pension, he had a stable income, but traditional banks turned him down due to his lack of credit history as a civilian.

Carlos turned to a community development financial institution (CDFI) specializing in supporting veterans.

With the microloan he received, Carlos opened "Carlos's Corner Store," a place where neighbors could buy essentials and catch up over a cup of coffee.

The store became a hub for the community, and Carlos's commitment to providing excellent service paid off.

His business thrived, and the microloan helped him turn his post-military entrepreneurial dream into a reality.

STORY 3: MARIA'S CATERING DELIGHTS

Maria, a talented chef, wanted to start her catering business, "Maria's Catering Delights."

She had a strong business plan but lacked the funds to purchase necessary kitchen equipment.

Maria applied for a microloan from an online lending platform that specialized in supporting culinary entrepreneurs.

With the microloan, Maria equipped her kitchen, and her catering business took off. Her delicious dishes and exceptional service became well-known in her community.

Not only did she repay her microloan, but she also expanded her business and started offering cooking classes.

Maria's story demonstrates how microloans can empower entrepreneurs in niche industries to achieve their dreams.

DIGITAL
TRANSFORMATION

STORY 4: JONATHAN'S DIGITAL DREAM

Jonathan had a passion for technology and dreamed of starting his digital marketing agency

However, he faced a unique challenge – he was a recent college graduate with student loans and no credit history.

Jonathan explored online lenders that catered to young entrepreneurs. With a microloan, Jonathan launched his digital marketing agency,

"DigitalDreams Co." He provided innovative solutions to small businesses looking to enhance their online presence.

Jonathan's business grew rapidly, and he not only repaid his microloan but also hired other young professionals, creating job opportunities in his community.

Jonathan's story is a testament to how microloans can empower young, aspiring entrepreneurs.

STORY 5: RACHEL'S ART STUDIO

Rachel, an artist with a deep passion for teaching, envisioned opening her art studio where she could offer art classes to children and adults.

However, her savings were limited, and traditional banks required significant collateral.

Rachel found a microloan program offered by a microfinance institution specializing in supporting creative entrepreneurs.

With the microloan, Rachel established "Rachel's Art Studio." Her art classes became popular, and she even offered scholarships to underprivileged children.

Her dedication to fostering creativity in her community not only repaid her microloan but also contributed to the cultural enrichment of her neighborhood.

Rachel's story illustrates how microloans can transform not only businesses but entire communities.

Decoding the Language of Microloans

We include a glossary to help you decode the language of microloans, ensuring you're well-versed in the terminology and concepts associated with microloan borrowing.

MICROLOANS GLOSSARY

- *Microloans:* Small-scale, short-term loans typically provided to small businesses, startups, and entrepreneurs.
- *Microlender:* A financial institution or organization that specializes in offering microloans to small businesses.
- *Interest Rate:* The percentage charged by the lender on the loan amount, representing the cost of borrowing.
- *Loan Amount:* The total sum of money borrowed from a microlender. Repayment Terms: The agreed-upon conditions for repaying the microloan, including interest rates and repayment schedule.
- *Application Process:* The steps involved in applying for a microloan, which may vary depending on the microlender.
- *Microfinance Institutions:* Specialized lenders focused on providing financial services to underserved communities and small businesses. *Online Lenders:* Lending platforms on the internet that offer microloans, often providing a convenient application process.

APPENDIX:
MICROLOANS GLOSSARY

- *Community Development Financial Institutions (CDFIs):* Organizations dedicated to lending to underserved communities and promoting economic development.
- *Business Plan:* A detailed document outlining a business's goals, strategies, and financial projections, often required by microlenders.
- *Credit Score:* A numerical representation of an individual's or business's creditworthiness, affecting eligibility for loans.
- Transparency: The quality of being open and clear about loan terms, fees, and interest rates, ensuring no hidden surprises for borrowers.
- *Accessibility:* The ease with which borrowers can access customer support and assistance during the lending process.
- *Loan Specialization:* The focus of a microlender on specific industries or types of loans, aligning with the borrower's needs.

These terms are essential for understanding the world of microloans and making informed financial

ADDITIONAL RESOURCES

A TOOLKIT FOR SMALL BUSINESS OWNERS

In this section, we provide you with a toolkit of resources to help you on your small business journey. From business planning templates to financial management tools, this toolkit is designed to support your business's growth.

RECOMMENDED READING: EXPLORE THE WORLD OF BUSINESS FINANCE

We recommend further reading to expand your knowledge of business finance, giving you a broader perspective on the financial aspects of small business management.

ADDITIONAL RESOURCES
TOOL KIT

To further support your journey, we've included an array of resources in the "Additional Resources" section.

This toolkit is designed to provide you with practical tools and information to enhance your business's growth.

From business planning templates to financial management tools, we want to empower you to make well-informed financial decisions and take your business to new heights.

ADDITIONAL RESOURCES
Small Business Administration (SBA)

> The SBA offers a wealth of resources for small business owners, including loan information, business planning tools, and guides on financial management.

Accion

> Accion is a nonprofit microlender that provides financial support and resources to small businesses. Explore their website for loan options and educational materials.

Kiva

> Kiva is a microloan platform that connects entrepreneurs with lenders worldwide. Learn how Kiva works and how it can benefit your small business.

SCORE

> SCORE is a nonprofit organization that provides free mentoring and educational resources to small business owners. Find a local SCORE chapter or access their online webinars and workshops.

National Association for the Self-Employed (NASE)

> NASE offers small business resources, including grants, webinars, and discounts on business services. Discover how NASE can support your entrepreneurial journey.

U.S. Department of the Treasury [Community Development Financial Institutions Fund (CDFI Fund)](#)

> Learn about the CDFI Fund and how it supports organizations that provide financing to underserved communities and small businesses.

[Small Business Development Centers (SBDCs)](#)

> SBDCs are dedicated to helping small businesses succeed. Locate your nearest SBDC for free business consulting, training, and resources.

Business Networking Groups

> Join local business networking groups to connect with other entrepreneurs, share experiences, and access valuable insights and opportunities.

Online Small Business Communities

> Participate in online forums and communities focused on small business ownership. Share your questions and experiences with like-minded individuals.

Microloans Mastery Toolkit

> Access our exclusive toolkit, including templates, checklists, and guides to help you navigate the world of microloans effectively. From crafting a business plan to finding the right microlender, this toolkit has you covered.

These resources are designed to provide you with the tools, knowledge, and support you need to thrive as a small business owner, especially when exploring the world of microloans.

Whether you're looking for templates, expert guidance, or networking opportunities, you'll find valuable assistance within these options.